JUNIOR SURVIVAL LIBRARY

Smooth scaly and successful

THE SNAKE

Mike Linley

ANGLIA
Television Limited

Boxtree

Key to abbreviations

lb	pound
kg	kilogram
in	inch
ft	foot
yd	yard
cm	centimetre
m	metre
km	kilometre
sq mile	square mile
sq km	square kilometre
kph	kilometres per hour
mph	miles per hour

First published in 1990 by Boxtree Limited
Copyright © 1990 Survival Anglia Limited
Text copyright © 1990 Mike Linley

Front jacket photographs:
Survival Anglia/Mike Linley (Yellow eyelash viper)
Survival Anglia/Jeff Foot (Prairie rattlesnake)
Back jacket photograph:
Survival Anglia/Mike Linley (Sea snake)

Line drawings by Raymond Turvey

British Library Cataloguing in Publication Data
Linley, Mike
  The snake.
  1. Snakes.
  I. Title II. Series
  597.96

ISBN 1-85283-058-1

Edited by Miranda Smith
Designed by Groom & Pickerill
Typeset by Rowland Phototypesetting Limited
Bury St Edmunds, Suffolk

Printed and bound in Italy
by OFSA S.p.A.

For Boxtree Limited,
36 Tavistock Street,
London WC2E 7PB

Contents

What is a snake? 4

The legless lizard 6

Snakes worldwide 8

Movement 10

Detecting food 12

Killing prey 14

Swallowing prey 16

Courtship and mating 18

Egg-laying snakes 20

Bearing live young 22

Growth and change 24

Defence against predators 26

Snakes and man 28

Glossary and Notes on Author 30

Index 31

Acknowledgement 32

What is a snake?

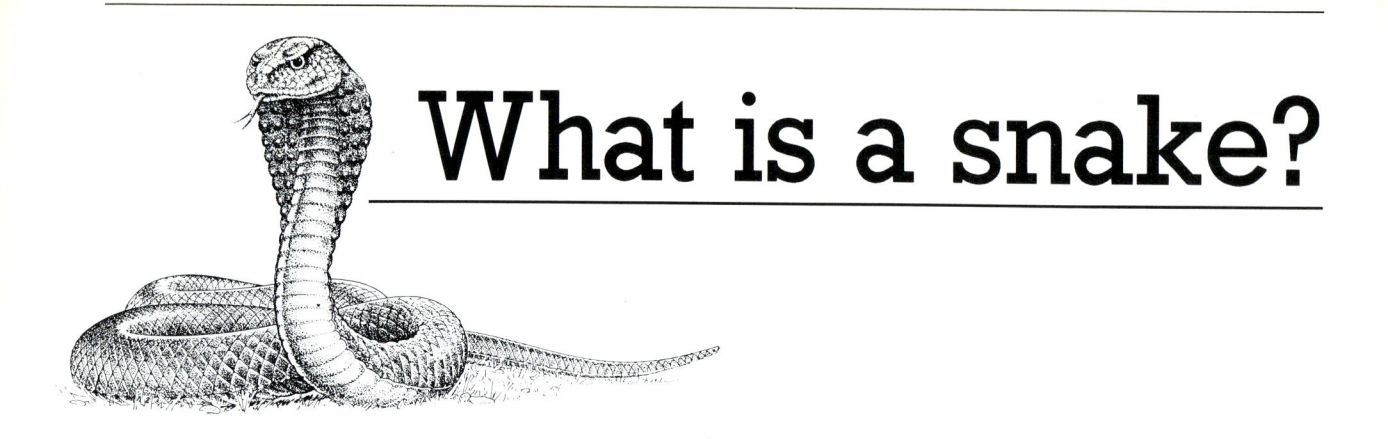

Apart from spiders, snakes are the most feared animals on earth. Many people believe that all snakes are **venomous**. In fact, only a comparatively small number of snakes have a dangerous bite; the vast majority are completely harmless. Even the most venomous do not attack often. The record for a man staying in a cage full of venomous snakes is 60 days and in all that time he was not bitten once.

Snakes are a highly successful group of animals that have existed for around 135 million years. They belong to the reptile family which includes lizards, crocodiles and turtles, and are the living relatives of dinosaurs. Like all reptiles, snakes are cold-blooded creatures that have scaly skins and breathe with lungs.

Unlike warm-blooded creatures, snakes do not produce their own body heat. Instead, they rely on the sun for warmth, which is why more are found in warm **tropical** regions than in cool, **temperate** areas.

A snake has no limbs and its body, up to half of which can be tail, is long and thin. Inside the muscles and ribs there are all the normal organs – the heart, intestines, lungs, liver and kidneys. However, the unusual

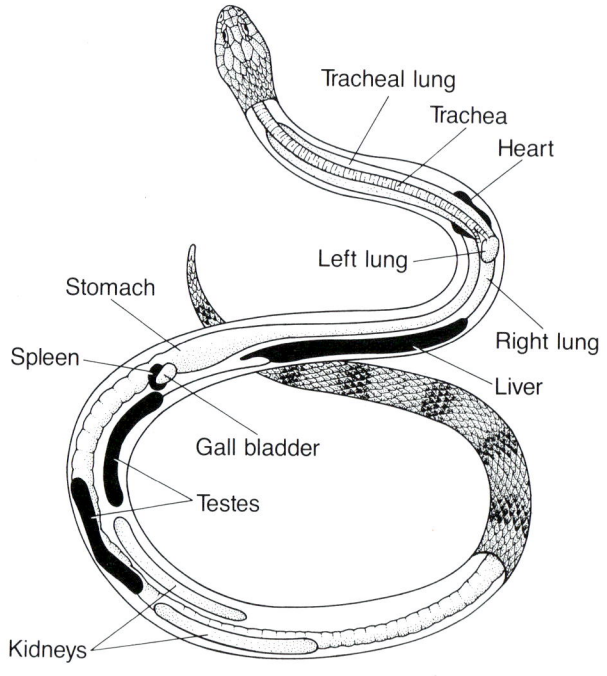

Below *The snake's body is covered in tough scales.*

Right *The position and shape of the snake's internal organs.*

Snakes have long, muscular bodies up to half of which may be tail.

shape of the body means that some of these organs have a different shape or position. Instead of being placed side by side, one kidney lies in front of the other. Also, in most species the left lung is either very small or missing, while the right lung is long and thin.

Although a snake has no ears, it can feel vibrations through its underside and could detect human footsteps approaching. With this kind of warning, it can make its escape. A snake does not have eyelids, its eyes are protected by clear, tough scales which means that it cannot blink. Many snakes have quite good eyesight but only over short distances.

A snake has a poor sense of smell but a strong sense of taste. Minute traces of chemicals are picked up on the end of its flicking tongue, either from the air or the ground. It is a very sensitive system for finding food, water, a mate, or giving warning of a **predator**.

The body of a snake is covered by tough scales. These act as a protective armour against the rocks and rough ground as the snake moves along. The scales are also a watertight covering to keep in moisture.

The legless lizard

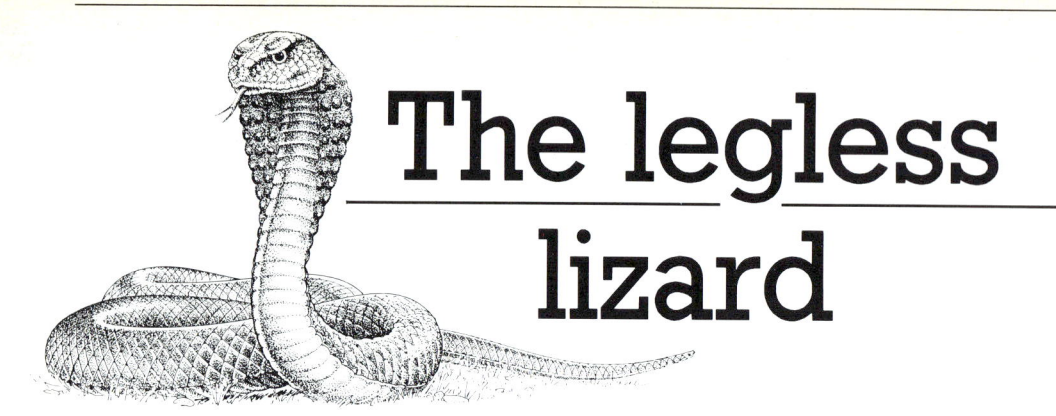

Snakes and lizards are closely related so it is very easy to confuse a snake with one of the many types of legless lizards. In fact, snakes probably **evolved** from lizards that gradually, over millions of years, lost their limbs and moved underground.

Many snakes such as boas and pythons still show signs that their ancestors once had limbs. This kind of snake has the remains of the hind limb bones inside its body. The only outward sign is a large claw on either side of the snake's **vent**. The claws appear to have no particular use. However, in some species they are larger in the male than in the female and are sometimes used during courtship.

While some snakes have the remains of legs, there are some lizards that are limbless and

Snakes do not have eyelids and are therefore unable to blink.

At first sight the slow-worm looks like a snake. In fact it is a legless lizard.

look just like snakes at first sight. The European slow-worm is an example. It has a long, smooth, scaly body and no trace of any limbs. It moves in the same way as a snake and uses its tongue to 'taste' its way. It does, however, have one feature that instantly sets it apart from a snake – eyelids. Although its eyes are very small, the slow-worm can blink, something no snake can do.

Like many other lizards, the slow-worm can also shed its tail if threatened by a predator. The muscles inside it twitch and cause the tail to wriggle for some time after it is shed. Hopefully, the reptile can then escape while the predator eats the tail. A new tail eventually grows, although it is never quite as perfect as the original. There are one or two species of snake that can also lose small sections of their tail in time of danger. However, the sections never regrow and if a snake loses a piece it is probably as the result of an accident rather than a deliberate means of escape.

There are other differences between snakes and legless lizards. Lizards have an ear opening, and the largest legless lizard is just over 1 m (3 ft) long. The largest snake is over ten times this length.

Snakes worldwide

There are nearly 2,400 known species of snake found throughout the world. They are very successful at adapting to almost every type of **habitat** except the polar regions. There are water snakes, sea snakes, burrowing snakes, tree snakes, desert-dwelling snakes and cave-living snakes.

Pythons are among the world's largest snakes. Some can measure up to 10 m (33 ft) long.

There is a far greater variety of species of snakes that live in the warmer regions of the world. This is because snakes are cold-blooded and need the sun's rays to keep warm. Hot tropical rainforests are home to many snakes, as are the desert regions of Australia, Africa and North America.

However, some snakes can survive in very cold environments. They do this by being active only at the warmer times of the year, and by spending much of their time sunbathing. The European adder lives within the cold Arctic Circle in Scandinavia. A type of pit viper is found at over 4,500 m (14,400 ft) in the Himalayas. The only areas of the world that do not have snakes at all are the North and South Poles, Ireland, Iceland, New Zealand and a few smaller remote islands.

Snakes vary in size from the tiny, burrowing snakes that are less than 15 cm (6 in) long to the enormous reticulated python that is said to reach a size of around 10 m (33 ft). All snakes feed on animals, and many species are equipped with **venom sacs** and **fangs** for killing their prey.

Flying snakes

The flying snake, found in the jungles of South-east Asia, is one of the most expert of tree climbers. It travels up and down lianas and trees at great speed, flattening its coils sideways against the surface. In order to travel from tree to tree the snake 'flies' through the air. It flattens out its body and draws it into S-shaped coils. In this way it glides to the next branch.

Some snakes are so small that they are sometimes confused with earthworms.

Movement

Although snakes have no limbs, they are able to move around with great ease and in many different ways. Some snakes are built to travel best on land, some under water, some in trees and some under loose sand. Most move by twisting the body from side to side in S-bends, pushing each coil against rocks, plants or simply against the ground. This is typical 'serpentine' movement, as practised by almost all snakes.

Heavy-bodied snakes like pythons and vipers use 'rib-walking'. The large belly scales of these snakes overlap backwards like a row of roof tiles. Sections of the body are raised, moved forward and then pushed against the ground, inching the snake forward in a straight line. This rib-walking is quite a slow method of travel and if the snake needs to move some distance in a hurry it has to resort to the serpentine movement.

The sidewinder can move easily over loose sand, leaving tell-tale tracks behind.

Ripples on the sand

Perhaps the strangest of all snake locomotion is that of the sidewinder, a type of rattlesnake from North America, and the sidewinding viper of the Namib Desert in south-west Africa.

These two snakes are not closely related, but they do share the same type of habitat – rolling dunes of loose sand. It is difficult terrain for a legless animal to cross, but both snakes have solved the problem in the same unique way.

The sidewinder throws its head and body in a series of loops over the sand so that only part of its body is touching the ground at any one time. The snake leaves behind very distinctive tracks in the sand.

Some snakes have a very specialized means of moving about. Tree snakes have an incredibly long, thin body that is often over 1 m (3 ft) in length, and yet not much thicker than a pencil. This shape helps them to blend in with

The African green tree snake can move through the branches at great speed.

the branches, and also means that the snakes can stretch through the air with no support for about two thirds of their body length in order to reach the next branch.

Some burrowing snakes move by contracting and expanding their body like a concertina. Earthworms move in this way too. Sea snakes spend their entire life under water and have bodies that are flattened like the tail fin of a fish. This helps them swim as they wriggle through the sea.

Detecting food

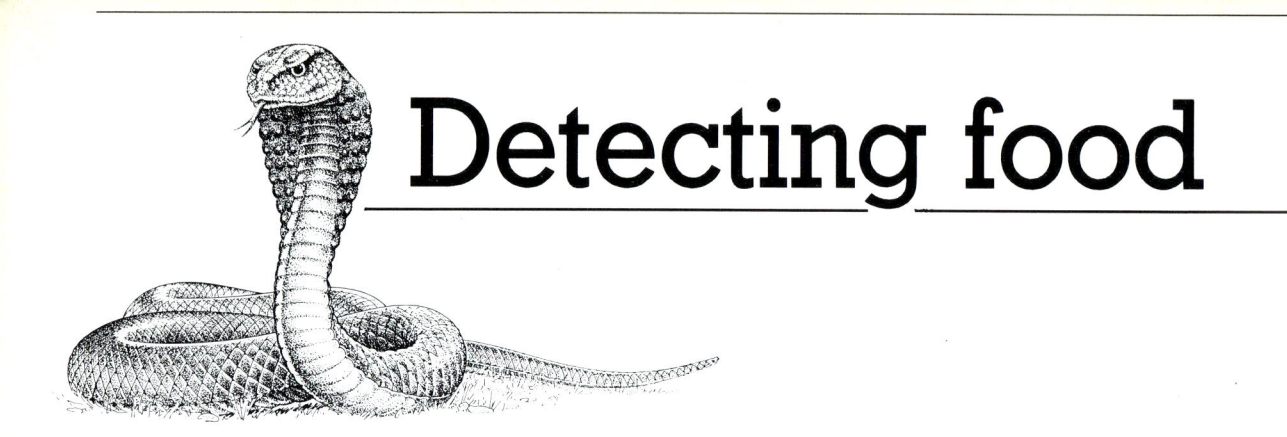

Snakes are hunters. They nearly all feed on living prey. This, depending on the snake, can be insects, fish, **amphibians**, reptiles – including other snakes – birds and mammals. Some species have a varied diet and eat almost any type of animal they come across. Others have a very particular diet. There are snakes that feed only on termites. Others eat only lizards or frogs or fish, and some simply birds' eggs. The king cobra eats only other snakes, and certain tree snakes from Central America feed on snails.

Some snakes sit and wait for their prey to get close, and rely on their own **camouflage** to remain unseen until they are ready to strike. Other snake species are active hunters and climb trees, enter burrows or search through the undergrowth until they disturb their prey.

Most snakes track their prey by sight. However, some use scent. As they flick their tongues in and out, they pick up minute traces

The horned viper lies beneath the sand and waits for prey to pass by.

The tree snake hunts for birds and lizards among the branches.

in the atmosphere or from the ground. These are detected by the sensitive Jacobson's organs that are in the roof of the snake's mouth. This helps snakes to find prey at night or inside a hollow log or burrow.

Certain rattlesnakes, vipers and pythons can track down the warm-blooded prey by sensing the heat which comes from their bodies. These snakes have special heat-detecting organs, called pit organs, either between the eye and nostrils or around the mouth of the reptile. Pit organs are very sensitive to slight differences in temperature. This means that even if the snake cannot see or smell its prey, it can detect the prey's body heat, home in on it, strike and catch it.

There are also one or two snakes, like a young fer-de-lance, that have brightly coloured tails that they wriggle in order to attract the attention of lizards or frogs. As a victim moves in to investigate, the snake strikes.

Killing prey

Snakes cannot chew, they have to swallow their prey whole. Some, like the garter snake, feed on frogs, toads and fish which are simply seized and swallowed alive. But most snakes kill their larger prey first.

In venomous species, it is the poison that, once injected into the body of the prey, causes **paralysis** or death. Snake venoms are often designed to deal with a particular type of prey. So the venom of a frog-eating snake works best on amphibians, while that of a bird-eater kills birds quickly. Some venoms act on the blood and heart while others attack the nerves. There are snakes whose venom works in both ways.

The faster acting the venom is, the sooner the prey stops moving. This means that the

A bush snake siezes a gecko in its jaws. Despite its size, the gecko will be swallowed whole.

snake has only to travel a short distance to actually capture its dying victim. Once inside the prey's body, the poison helps to break down the tissues and internal organs. This helps the process of **digestion** of the animal once it has been swallowed.

Many snakes kill their prey by **constriction**. This does not mean, as many people think, that the animal is crushed to death. A snake like a python will seize an animal in its jaws and then throw coils of its body around it. The reptile then begins to squeeze and so prevents the animal from breathing. In other words, the prey is simply suffocated. Snakes have very powerful and muscular bodies and once an animal has been seized it does not often escape.

Snakes only kill when they are hungry. They do not kill an animal and then return to it later. Very often, if a snake comes across a nest of young birds or mammals it can be swallowing one animal while constricting another in its coils.

Garter snakes swallow small fish and frogs whole, without killing them first.

Swallowing prey

Once a snake has caught its prey it then has to swallow it. Snakes swallow food whole, usually head first. It is easier that way because of the shape of the prey's head and the way its limbs fold flat against its body.

Snakes can swallow animals much larger in **diameter** than themselves. The African egg-eating snake can swallow a small hen's egg whole even though its own body is thinner than a man's finger. A python with a body the same diameter as a drainpipe is able to swallow an animal as big as a medium-sized dog. Snakes are able to do this because of the way in which the bones in their heads are organized.

Once an animal has been subdued by venom or constriction, the snake takes it into its mouth. The lower jaw has two halves. Each half moves forward in turn so that the jaw works its way along the victim's body. By twisting the neck and the coils of its body, the snake forces the animal down its throat and into its stomach.

One animal may last the reptile several days or even weeks. During this time the reptile often hides away because having such a large meal inside it makes movement very difficult. Everything is digested – in the case of an antelope, even the hooves and horns.

The African python will only swallow its prey once it has been constricted.

The African egg-eating snake can swallow birds' eggs larger than its own head.

Quadrate bone

SNAKE JAW OPEN

The snake's gape

The two halves of a snake's lower jaw are not joined at the front. Instead, they are only loosely connected by muscles and ligaments that can stretch apart. The jaw bones are attached in exactly the same way to either side of the skull. Not only can each lower jaw stretch away from the rest of the snake's skull, but the two halves can pull apart at the front of the reptile's mouth (see diagram on the left). The skin around the mouth and neck is very elastic too. All this means that the snake can swallow surprisingly large animals.

Below *The emerald tree boa, like most snakes, swallows its prey head first.*

17

Courtship and mating

Snakes normally live alone, so in order to breed they have to go in search of a mate. Their eyes are good at detecting movement, but they see little else. They do not rely on bright colours, crests, displays, calls or noises to attract a mate. Instead, it is their sense of smell that plays an important part in tracking down other snakes.

Prairie rattlesnakes mate when they emerge from their winter dens.

Once a male snake has found a female, he moves his head up and down her body, testing her scent with his tongue to judge whether or not she is ready to mate. Mating may last anything from just a few minutes to a period of several hours.

Some of the courtship and mating habits of snakes are very unusual. The American garter snake, like many species, goes into **hibernation** through the cold winter months. When the weather gets warmer, the males emerge

Adders mate in late spring. The male is the brighter of the two.

from the hibernation dens in huge numbers and wait at the entrances. As the females emerge, the males find them by scent and mate with them. The sight of these snakes can be spectacular – hundreds, often thousands of reptiles wriggling around in an area only a few metres square.

The 'mating dance' of the common viper and American rattlesnakes was thought to be part of the courtship ritual. However, it only takes place between males, and is probably the way these snakes see off a rival. The snakes raise the front part of their bodies up in the air and twist around each other, trying to force their rival to the ground. Every so often they push so hard that they spring apart. It is a trial of strength, and the loser quickly disappears into the undergrowth.

One species of snake does not need to find a mate at all. The blind burrowing snake of Asia is female. Males are completely unknown. This tiny snake, smaller than a pencil, lives in loose, dry earth. She simply lays eggs that hatch into more females. This method of reproduction is known as parthenogenesis. In the reptile world, only this snake and a few lizards are known to breed like this.

19

Egg-laying snakes

Some species of snake lay eggs while others give birth to live, fully-formed young. The egg shell of a snake is not hard and chalky like that of a bird; instead it is tough and leathery. After the egg has been laid it soaks up water from the surrounding earth and may increase in size by up to 50 per cent. Depending on the species, a snake can lay anything from 2–40 eggs, but the average **clutch** size is 15–20 eggs.

The eggs are usually laid under logs, in holes in the ground or in tussocks of grass. Some snakes lay them in heaps of vegetation so that the heat given off by the rotting leaves helps to warm the clutch and speed up the

Breaking out

Breaking out of the egg is an exhausting business for a hatchling snake. It has a tiny 'egg-tooth' at the end of its snout which it uses to slash its way out of the leathery shell. It may have to slash the egg many times before it succeeds in making an opening. The hatchling then sits with only its head showing, often for several hours, before it emerges completely.

A day or two after hatching, the snake sheds its skin for the first time. It also loses the egg-tooth, and leaves the area of the nest to hunt for its first meal.

Spitting cobras often lay their eggs inside termite mounds.

growth of the young snakes inside. Other species lay their eggs inside termite mounds where they benefit from the warmth and protection of the mound.

Most snakes do not look after their offspring at all. Once the eggs have been laid, the female often simply leaves them. There are one or two species though that do remain with the clutch. The female king cobra actually builds a nest for her eggs out of leaves and grass. The clutch is put in a hole near the top of the pile and then covered over. She remains coiled on top of the nest on guard until they are ready to hatch.

A hatchling grass snake rips through the tough egg shell with a special egg-tooth.

Some pythons also coil around their eggs. The Indian python actually twitches while wrapped around the egg to produce small amounts of heat in her muscles, which helps to **incubate** the clutch. This is the only species of reptile known to act in this way.

The eggs of most species of snake take two or three months to hatch, depending on the temperature. Some snakes lay their eggs with the **embryo** already well developed inside and these may hatch in only two or three weeks.

Bearing live young

In some species of snake, the eggs are kept inside the body until they are ready to hatch. There are two advantages in this. Firstly, many snake eggs are taken by predators such as raccoons and wild pigs. By keeping the eggs inside her body, the female snake can protect them. Secondly, by carrying them around, she acts as a mobile incubator. She can go and sit in nice sunny positions to increase her body temperature and so warm up the eggs.

As there is no need for a tough, leathery skin to protect the eggs, the embryos develop inside a thin, transparent **membrane**. The young snakes are born inside these individual sacs, and break free moments later. Usually, as soon as the young emerge from the sacs, they disappear into the undergrowth to live independent lives. Some species however, like the European asp, may remain with her 12 or so young for several days to protect them.

There are many different snakes that are **ovoviviparous**, or give birth to living young. They include boas, vipers, some water snakes and all sea snakes. Sea snakes rarely come ashore and their eggs would not develop underwater. Giving birth to live young is therefore the only way they can reproduce.

The adder is the only species of snake that is found inside the Arctic Circle. It produces live young each summer because it is so cold where it lives. If it laid eggs they would simply never hatch. The only other reptile to share its habitat, the common lizard, gives birth to live young for the same reason.

Giving birth in this way does not necessarily limit the number of offspring a snake can have. The African puff adder may produce between 70 and 100 young in a single batch. The North American garter snake regularly has litters of around 50 young.

Right *The rainbow boa from Central and South America may have twelve or more live young.*

Above *The sand boa gives birth to four or five live young.*

Above *A large puff adder may give birth to over 70 young at a time.*

23

Growth and change

Newly hatched or newly born snakes are simply miniature copies of the adult snake. Some are more brightly coloured when young. Others are more camouflaged than their parents so that they do not fall prey to predators. The young of the green tree python from Papua New Guinea are not in fact green, but bright yellow or orange. They gradually change colour as they grow.

All snakes are completely independent from birth and have to hunt for their own living prey. The young of venomous species are born with the venom sacs and venom ready for use.

Because the hatchling snake is so much smaller than the adult, many have to start life feeding on a different type of prey. Many species of snake that feed almost entirely on

Above *The snake's skin is usually shed in one whole piece.*

Opposite *Just before shedding, the snake's transparent eyeshields become cloudy.*

mammals or birds as adults will take small lizards or frogs when young. The young of some small types of snake may even catch spiders or centipedes.

The rate at which a snake grows depends on the weather and how available its food is. Snakes can go for months, even years, without feeding, but during this time they do not grow at all. In captivity, some well fed pythons can grow from around 45 cm (17½ in) to over 2 m (6½ ft) in a year.

The scales on a snake's body are covered in **keratin**. In order to grow, this hard layer has from time to time to be shed or **sloughed off**. In the case of lizards, the skin flakes off in pieces. With snakes it is usually shed in one single piece that rolls off the body, like a sock being turned inside out, as the snake moves through the undergrowth. When the skin comes off, it reveals new, slightly larger scales that have already formed underneath.

The first sign that a snake is about to slough is that its eyes turn **opaque** for a few days as the new protective shields are being formed. As well as enabling the snake to grow, shedding its skin also allows the snake to replace any damaged scales and rid itself of any mites or ticks.

Defence against predators

Many animals feed on snakes. The mongoose is one of the most famous of the snake's enemies along with the secretary bird of Africa. There are also snake-eating eagles in Southern Europe and Africa. So it is important that snakes are able to defend themselves.

When threatened, most snakes will hiss loudly, and some may even strike at whatever is threatening them. Although snake venom is designed mainly for killing prey, many venomous snakes will bite an attacker and cause severe pain, sometimes even death.

Apart from biting, different species have a variety of ways of defending themselves. The rattle in the tail of the rattlesnake evolved so that large animals like buffalo could hear the snake and so avoid stepping on it. If this warning fails, then the snake resorts to striking. Instead of biting, the spitting cobra sprays venom into the eyes of a predator. Its fangs are hollow with a hole in the front of the tooth. By applying pressure on the venom sac, the snake can spit very accurately over a distance of 1–2 m (3–6 ft). The poison is very powerful and causes intense pain and even blindness.

The grass snake, like many species, gives off a foul-smelling odour if attacked. This is

If cornered, the spitting cobra can spray venom into the eyes of a predator.

Hidden from view

Some snakes rely on their camouflage to avoid being seen. Tree snakes and vine snakes have long, very thin bodies. They move slowly through the branches, often swaying as if blown by the wind. They look just like part of the plant they are climbing, so they not only avoid being seen but can also sneak up on lizards and other prey.

The gaboon viper from Central Africa is a large, heavy-bodied snake that is marked to blend in perfectly with the fallen leaves on the forest floor. Despite its large size – it can reach almost 2 m (6½ ft) in length – it is almost impossible to see until it moves.

Above *The bright colours of the coral snake warn predators that it is highly venomous.*

Below *Vine snakes are well camouflaged in the trees where they live.*

often enough to put off a predator. Sometimes the grass snake may even pretend to be dead by rolling on its back and lying with its mouth open and tongue hanging out. Many predators are only interested in living, not dead, prey and so leave the snake alone.

Some venomous species, like the coral snakes, are brightly banded red, yellow and black to warn animals not to try and attack them. Some harmless species are marked in exactly the same way as the venomous ones. They too are left in peace by predators.

27

Snakes and man

Man has always had a fear of snakes whether venomous or not. In many parts of the world, snakes are still killed by man on sight, even though only a tiny percentage of them can be regarded as dangerous. However, it is easy to understand why snakes are so feared. In those countries where there is little medical help, which can itself be many miles away a bite from a venomous snake can mean death.

In India alone, it has been estimated that between 25,000 and 35,000 people die each year from snakebite. In the United States, where the annual death toll from snake bites rarely exceeds 20, huge numbers of rattlesnakes are hunted each year and killed, skinned and sometimes eaten in 'Rattlesnake round-ups'.

Venom is pumped out of a rattlesnake by squeezing the venom sacs above the mouth.

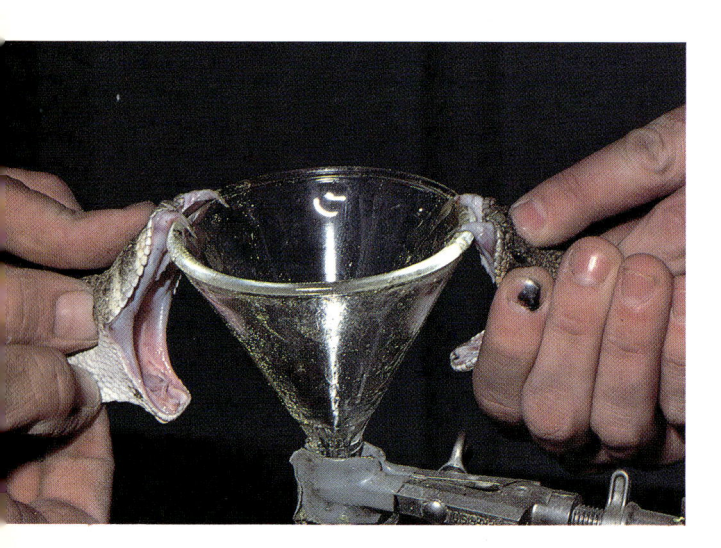

Above *Huge numbers of rattlesnakes are rounded up and slaughtered each year in Texas.*

Snakes are eaten by many people in different parts of the world. In China and Hong Kong, snakes are sold in markets for food and medicinal use. It is difficult to understand how eating a snake's gall bladder can cure a headache, but recent scientific work has shown that snakes can be of great benefit to medicine. It may be that snake venom can help people suffering from diseases of the nervous system. Research is also being carried out on the skin of sea snakes that may prove useful in treating people who have been badly burned.

Many snakes also have an important role to play in their natural environment. Many are very important in controlling pests. The majority of snakes feed on rodents such as mice and rats. If we continue to kill snakes for food, their skin, sport or just out of fear, then there would be a serious problem with the growing numbers of mice and rats in these countries.

If left undisturbed, almost all snakes quietly move off and disappear into the undergrowth, avoiding all contact. Snakes are far more afraid of us than we are of them.

A snake charmer sways his pipe to attract the attention of the cobra.

Snake charming

In India and North America, snake-charmers have entertained travellers for centuries with their snakes, usually cobras. They appear from baskets and sway to the sound of the charmer's music.

In fact, snakes are almost completely deaf and certainly cannot hear the sound of the music. They simply react to the swaying pipe which is shaped and marked like another cobra.

Glossary

Amphibians Animals that live both on land and in water, for example frogs and newts.

Camouflage The ability to hide from an enemy by appearing to be part of the natural background.

Clutch The total number of eggs laid by a snake at one time.

Constriction The tightening of a snake's coils around its victim to prevent it from breathing.

Diameter The width of a circle.

Digestion The process by which the body breaks down substances and absorbs them.

Embryo The developing animal within an egg or inside the body of a snake.

Evolved Slowly developed and changed over many thousands or millions of years.

Fangs The enlarged teeth of a snake used to inject venom.

Habitat The environment in which an animal usually lives.

Hibernation The period of inactivity or sleep that creatures like bears or snakes go through during the cold, winter months.

Incubate To warm eggs so that they develop and hatch.

Keratin A tough substance that strengthens nails, hair, horns and hooves.

Membrane A thin sheet of skin or tissue.

Ovoviviparous A snake that keeps the eggs within its body until they are ready to hatch, so giving birth to live young.

Opaque Dull, so that light cannot be seen through the object.

Paralysis The loss of the ability to move.

Predator An animal that lives by preying on other animals.

Slough off Shed or cast off skin.

Temperate The regions of the earth between the tropics and the ice caps with moderate temperatures.

Tropical The warmer regions of the earth near the equator.

Venomous Poisonous, having a liquid that, injected into prey, will kill or overpower it.

Venom sacs The sacs that produce and store venom.

Vent A single opening between the snake's body and tail.

About the author

Mike Linley has had a keen interest in reptiles and amphibians since the age of four, and this is his sixth book on the subject. Mike has a B.Sc. Hons degree in Zoology from Durham University and after teaching for three years he went to Bristol University to research lizard behaviour. He now works for Survival Anglia as a producer of natural history documentaries for the long-running Survival series and presents the Anglia Television children's series ANIMALS IN ACTION.

Index

The entries in **bold** are illustrations.

adders 9, 22
   African puff 22, **22–3**

boas 6, 22
   emerald **17**
   sand **23**
breathing 4
burrowing snakes 8, 9, 11, 19
bush snakes **14**

camouflage 12, 24, 26, 30
claws 6
cobras **29**
   king 12, 21
   spitting 20, 26, **26**
coral snakes 27, **27**
courtship 18–19

earthworms 11
egg-eating snakes **16**
   African **16**
European asp 22
European slow-worm 6–7, **7**
eyelids **6**, 7, **25**

fangs 9, 30
fer-de-lance 13
flying snakes 9

gape 16, 17, **17** 30
garter snakes 14, **15**, 18
   American 18, 22
grass snakes **21**, 26–7

habitat 8, 10, 22, 30
hatchlings 20–1, 22–3, 24–5
   egg-teeth 20, 21
   independence 24

hibernation 18, 30
   dens 18, **18**
Himalayas 9
hissing 26
hunting 12, 20

Internal organs **4**

Jacobson's organs 13
Jaw **17**

lizards 4, 6–7, 19, 22

mating 18–19
mites 25

Namib Desert 10
nests 21

ovoviviparous snakes 20, 30

parthenogenesis 19
pit organs 13
predators 24, 26–7
   man 28–9
   mongeese 26
prey 12–13, 14–15, 24–5, 26
   antelope 16
   birds 12, 14, 15
   birds' eggs 12, **16**
   constriction of 15, **16** 30
   digestion of 16
   fish 12, 14, **15**
   frogs and toads 12, 13, 14, **15**
   insects 12
   lizards 12, 13, **14**, 26
   mammals 12, 15
   reptiles 12

snails 12
swallowing of 16, **16** 17, **17**
termites 12
pythons 6, **8**, 10, 13, 15, 16, 25
   African **16**
   green tree 24
   Indian 21
   reticulated 9

rattlesnakes 13, 19, 26, 28, **28**
   prairie **18**
   rattle of 26
reptiles 4
rib-walking 10

scales 4, **4**, 5, 10, 25
   keratin in 25, 30
sea snakes 8, 11, 22, 29
senses 12, 13
   hearing 5
   sight 5, 18, 19
   smell 18
   taste 5
skin, shedding of 20, **24**, 25, **25**
sidewinder 10, **10**
snake-charming 29, **29**
snakes
   as prey 28
   controlling pests 29
snake's eggs 20–1
   as food 22
   hatching of 20
   incubation of 20–1, 22, 30

spiders, fear of 4
sun-bathing 9

tails 5, 26
  shedding of 7
tree snakes 8, 10–11, **11**, **13**
trials of strength 19

venom 4, 14–15, 26, 27, 28, **28**, 30
  as medicine 28
venom sacs 9, 24, 30
vent 6, 30
vine snakes **27**

vipers 13, 19, 22
  common 19
  gaboon 26
  horned **12**
  pit 9

water snakes 8, 22

Picture Acknowledgements

The publishers would like to thank the
Survival Anglia picture library
and the following photographers for the use
of photographs on the pages listed:

Andy Bee 4; Alan Root 5,11,16,17,20,26; Liz Bomford 7;
Jen & Des Bartlett 6,15; Goetz Dieter Plage 8; Dr F. Koster 9;
Mike Linley 10,21,27,28; Michael Kavanagh 13;
Jeff Foott 12, 18,24,25,28; Jan Teede 14; Bruce Davidson 15,16,23;
Maurice Tibbles 19; Keith & Liz Laidler 22,23;
Mike Price 27; Joanna Van Gruisen 29.